Equal To Now

Samantha Hall

Front cover artwork - ArtbySamHall

This book is dedicated to
all who have shared their encouragement
- meditators and non-meditators alike -
and to the beauty of life which inspired it

Introduction

I first met Samantha in 2018 and could see very clearly there was a genuine yearning to discover life's truth.

It wasn't long until I learned she wrote poetry and on one of our retreats I suggested she read one out. I was amazed! The first one I heard was called *Surrender*...

"Like the plants surrender to the earth
the trees surrender to the breeze
No willpower required
just life living with ease..."

These words described exactly all that I set out to convey on the meditation retreat and with such clarity, simplicity and beauty.

On our extended retreats I often attempted to explain silence - why we have it, what it is and its benefits. However, I don't need to go into expanded explanations any longer, all I need to do is read Samantha's beautiful poem below, which points to the spirit of silence better than any discourse. On reading this I was stunned into silence myself!

The Stillness of Silence
When we trust in what we know
at one with our inner glow
the stillness of silence settles us so
Questioning all we perceive as real
abandoning commentary in order to feel

the stillness of silence helps us to heal

Releasing beliefs once held fast

no longer under the spell they cast

the stillness of silence embraces until at last

The doors of perception open wide

no sense of separation, no divide

the stillness of silence with our being collides

Resting in this place of knowing

aware of life, ebbing and flowing

the stillness of silence is us, love growing

The words at the end of the second stanza are full of insight and wonder: *"abandoning commentary in order to feel, the stillness of silence helps us to heal"*. Healing, we could say, is what meditation, silence, going on retreats is all about. Not just emotional healing but the deeper healing found in the last stanza: *"The doors of perception open wide, no sense of separation, no divide."* Through meditation and silence we heal the division not only between ourselves and others, but between ourselves and life itself, because there is only One and we are all it.

What is most striking about Samantha's poems is the depth with which they convey the eternal presence that is everything, by stirring that "place" beyond the thinking analytical mind. In such a few words she can touch the fabric of non-dual reality, allowing you – if only for a moment - to taste it for yourself.

Suryacitta, The Happy Buddha

CONTENT

We Are Here

Like 20:20 vision, everything is clear
when all of life's experiences we choose to hold dear

No labels of good or bad to adhere
no reactions inside to the voices that jeer

Sights to behold, sounds to our ear
all senses alert and in top gear

Real emotion in the drop of a tear
or expressed as a heart-rending cheer

Don't pick and choose, keep it all near
life is an experience to love not fear

Be with the simple knowing – We Are Here

Really ....

It's only when we tune out the chatter
in the silence, we discover the things that matter
and realise we're not really as mad as a Hatter

Those voices telling us all the things we are not
regurgitating pressures of the things not yet got
and how without them we'll never really be 'that hot'

There's only one voice we need to tune into
the inner one that wants us to be, not just do
and then we'll understand what really is true

We are enough, just the way we are
whether black, white, with a blemish or scar
and it's this knowledge that will really take us far

So within this conceptual time and space
let's explore all we are, in that inner place
and really move forward with compassion and grace

'cos life is to be experienced, right here and now
no fear, or questions, 'what me, but how?'
really be adventurous, time to step into life's 'WOW'

Rest In You

We all have those times, don't we?
when the distractions from now are constantly there
if not lost in the drama of the way it was
it's of the future and its when, why, where?

Well don't despair, there's still room for congratulations
'cos every time we notice, we are aware, we come back
to the senses and the anchor they offer
to this place of peace, where there's no sense of lack

Where the simplicity of life is truly seen
as we allow it to unfold unhindered
by our expectations, wants and limiting beliefs
and the need to cling and avoid are finally splintered

So next time you are having one of those times
remember a thought is only a thought
drop into the heart centre, get out of the head
rest in you, and in presence be caught

Feel It From The Start

Wake to each day, with gratitude in your heart
be thankful for loves presence, feel it from the start
the day will be what it will be
it's our awareness that determines what we see

We can experience it as it is, in the reality of now
or start with worrying, 'nexting', a permanently furrowed brow
one will bring peace and allowing to our day
the other self-suffering, from which it's hard to get away

We get lost in the fear and loathing, very often of ourselves
into all our faults destructive thinking delves
and if not us, we judge and criticise others
or blame our life's difficulties on our fathers and mothers

When they like us, only did what they knew
passing on thoughts and beliefs - not necessarily true
too much time spent in expectation, of what should or could be
missing out on life's beauty - here for all to see

For when we tune out the chatter and surrender to our senses
an unfolding occurs, bringing down our defences
a veil is lifted we can, at last, experience what's real
so become one with these senses and feel, feel, feel

Breathe In The Light

Breathe in the light
the loving light of who we are
Breathe out and release
sharing our light afar

When we notice we are no longer present
lost in thought, imagination, dreams
look for the light, it is always here
so much closer than it sometimes seems

Yes, it is always here, within us
hidden by the distractions, the wants and the noise
waiting with its gift - the present
ready to envelop us in its untold joys

Offering all that our senses can deliver
anchoring us, with their attributes, to the now
no thinking required in their presence
observing is all we need to allow

Breathe in the light
the loving light of who we are
Breathe out and release
sharing our light afar

All Illusions Shattered

As we sit in meditation
and practice mindfulness in everyday things
we find ourselves constantly returning
to our senses and all that this brings

sights, smells and touch – alert and in receipt
all drama and demands laid to rest
the sound of the traffic at one with the birds
and any sensation warmly hosted as our guest

in this space, there's no need for our story
simply at one with the breath – in and out
at ease with all we are in the moment
free from comparison, judgment and doubt

in this reality all illusions are shattered
THIS IS IT – there is no great reveal
no holy grail to hunt down, or hidden meaning
the inner knowledge, is simply to feel

and as we feel into our bodies and experience
all that's here with no outcome pre-set
the idea of separation – the biggest illusion
is so far from the connections we get

the connections come through in synchronicities

in nature and all of her gifts

in the smiling eyes of a stranger

in the shared suffering of attaining our shifts

no longer lost in over-thinking

of attaching to every emotion spent

we cultivate the art of being

in gratitude for this experience leant

No Willpower Required

In mindfulness we don't need willpower
no, it's willingness that's the name of the game
trying and striving won't cut it
noticing distractions from the present, is our aim

And that's where we need to be willing
to notice thoughts, sensations and to let them be
we then return to our breath and our senses
and it's this repetition which truly sets us free

We realise these things are not who we are
as we stay longer in the now, in our presence
simply thoughts to be acknowledged, sensations to be felt
no clinging or aversion in our true essence

So in time, we shed our expectations,
judgements, criticisms – all just thought
we learn afresh to truly love ourselves and others
and discover we are the peace we sought

Stillness Within

When we connect to the stillness within
we witness self-compassion begin
sitting with this stillness inside
there's no place for our feelings to hide

Sensations within give the feelings their form
swirling and building, like the eye of a storm
don't push away, experience it all
any tension, heat, the rise and the fall

'Resistance is futile' as the saying goes
self-denial one of our greatest foes
don't judge the feelings as they make themselves known
observe them, sense them, they're all self-grown

We learn to welcome them, be at one with their presence
love every part, of this, our true essence
witness the change, as it goes with the flow
experience the connection with our inner glow

Pause Awhile

Pause awhile and simply notice
the wonder of the breath – in and out
feel its progress moving through the body
life-affirming – without a doubt

Pause awhile and simply notice
the music all around – to hear
made by birds or even a whisper
as melodic as rumbling traffic changing gear

Pause awhile and simply notice
all the sights in front of the eyes
up close - or at a distance
even in the familiar there can be a surprise

Pause awhile and simply notice
any fragrances that hang in the air
maybe sweet - or perhaps pungent
inhale them all with no judgement to share

Pause awhile and simply notice
any taste in the mouth, on the tongue
lips savour, many a flavour
taste buds distinguishing mild from strong

Pause awhile and simply notice
the sense of touch, where the feet meet the ground
where fingers brush against one another
sensations, old and new, can be found

Pause awhile and simply notice
the thinking mind in overdrive
not needed on every occasion
in the chatter its true ability we deprive

Pause awhile and simply notice
the connection to peace and love we allow
by experiencing all in this moment
our presence in this here and this now

Cultivating Compassion

It begins with a little kindness
shown to ourselves - which is often rare
kindness tends to be saved for others
watching our thoughts the place to start, if we dare

The thoughts which tell us we're lacking
in looks, in money, in love
the thoughts not even of our own making
but still we let them dig, poke and shove

Dig and poke at our insecurities
shove us into boxes with labels fixed tight
but when we observe ourselves with kindness
self-compassion will set us right

By observing thoughts, feelings, emotions
and gratefully giving space to truly experience their ways
compassion expands to all the planet's inhabitants
bringing a fresh perspective and peace to our days

Praise It So

Courage to trust, to follow, to flow
Spurred on by love, as the whispers grow
Louder and clearer, from the seeds sown
Compassion and kindness in presence are known
Beauty, freedom and wonder on show
With gratitude and recognition, we praise it so

Experiencing Is King

Feel, connect, feel some more
    Gratitude grounds us to the core

Aware of the nervous system's memory clinging
in this knowledge comes freedom, the heart is singing

This kindness to allow all to arise
to be truly felt with no disguise

Aware of sensations before they fall
yes, this is the kindest kindness of all

Letting life be, without the push and pull
pleasant the master, unpleasantness to cull

Aware of life's nature, experiencing is King
be at one with this nature, release the suffering

Aware of all on offer, beyond must-haves and wants
rest in the inner wisdom - the heart's response

Feel, connect, feel some more
    Being this wonder brings love to the fore

This Here, This Now, This Present

This here, this now, this present
this gift of life - this direct mind-body experience
this feast for our senses

See it, hear it, smell it
taste it, touch it, feel it

live it, love it, be it

This here, this now, this present

Joyful in its simplicity
when experienced in its entirety
when not ruled by anxiety
or conforming to the demands of society
is the very testimony
of what can truly set us free

We Settle

We settle in silence and open our hearts
to all we are, beyond activity of mind
this connection to all, in our presence we abide
we are this knowing, compassionate and kind

We settle in stillness with our hearts awide
allowing thought and sensation to simply be
activities of life, observed, then let go
in this knowing we are free of the 'me'

We settle in presence, aware of life's flow
and any resistance we kindly release
back into the loving, cradling embrace
of our true self, in its wisdom and peace

Surrender

Like the plants surrender to the earth
the trees surrender to the breeze
no will power required
just life living, with ease

Like the clouds surrender to the sky
the oceans surrender to the tide
no striving, no effort
just life living, no aside

Like the tides surrender to the sun and the moon
the stars surrender to the night sky
no trying to change a thing
just life living, no reason why

Like the body surrenders to the breath
we too now surrender to our presence
no expectations, no assumptions
just life living, our aware essence

This Wonder-filled Life

The day goes by
and every blink of the eye
brings more wonders into focus

All that we hear
vibration at the inner ear
pure magic, no hocus-pocus

As we breathe in
the smell receptors begin
engaging with aromas in the air

Our fingers meet
rough or smooth, what a treat
to feel, without a care

Flavours on the tongue
like dancers to a song
come alive, more wonders unfold

Whilst the thinking mind
when quietened we find
is another sense to behold

Together these senses
connect us, no pretences
allowing both pleasure and strife

They are the anchor
to the peace we hanker
after this, our wonder-filled life

Presence

Awaken to a fresh new day
perfect in its simplicity
aware of synchronicity
connecting us, no duplicity
when the chattering mind falls away

Experience is the order of the day
feel it in its entirety
observe and release superiority
witness the ingenuity
when in our presence we learn to stay

Without ....

Love & gratitude for all on view
Without thought of what's yet to be seen

Appreciate all, here and now
Without thought of what might have been

Give yourself over to the task at hand
Without judgements of good and bad

Feel the sensations, one and all
Without siding with happy over sad

Sow the seeds of compassion and watch them grow
Without concern of could and should

Simply allow what is present to be as it is
Without ignoring love's call homeward

As Our Awareness Grows

"These things are sent to try us"
so the saying goes
but these things become less upsetting
as the awareness grows

Awareness grows through meditation
and expands as we take in the everyday
tasks which don't require our thinking
tasks in whose presence we stay

We stay aware through the gift of our senses
and in time, the longer in this presence we abide
the things once un-tolerated, griped over
seem smaller, have less hold, subside

Subside as we sit in meditation
and are at one with these everyday tasks
as we realise we are part of something much bigger
of who we are behind the masks

The masks of our name, our gender,
mother or father, child, orphan, sibling, friend
the masks of what we do for a living
all the masks that encourage us to pretend

To pretend our suffering is caused by anything
other than wanting things to be different from how they are
expectations, judgments, over-thinking
and our opinions - oh too many by far

By far, the biggest pretence of all
that we are separate, unconnected, alone
becomes apparent as we fall awake in meditation
and our oneness as all is simply known

Life's Dance

Let love and compassion be the arena of life's dance
as we move to its rhythm, not holding fast to one stance

Have the courage to feel everything, every sway, lift and spin
and never see the pauses and rests as a sin

Co-existence on its dance floor, all emotion we bring
joy and sadness, frustration, laughter – the music of life, living

Be Still

The breath followed gently
reconnects us with now
with the simplicity of life in this moment

The heart beats at will
no control, no command
only a gratitude for this, life's bestowment

Acknowledge each breath
with respect and thanks
for all that it gives unbidden

Follow it lightly
no push and pull
to see what, in its depths, is hidden

Observe with an open heart
aware of expectation and want
as the day unfolds at will

Notice with neutrality
all that arises and falls
and in this given peace and silence, be still

Rest In The Middle

With each life-affirming breath
flowing in and flowing out
we ground, centre, align

We observe life for what it is
as it flows and unfolds
beyond the idea of me and mine

Thought will distract us
with rumination on the past
and pull us this way and that

Predictions of a future
over-planned yet unknown
imagined, no basis in fact

So rest in the middle
rest here in now
rest in the middle as thou

Naturally

Trust the process
the process of life living
observe all as it unfolds

Naturally, like the body breathing - following its own rhythm

Naturally, like the river - following its own course

Naturally, like the waves - moving with the current

Naturally, like the trees - moving with the breeze

Naturally, like the day –
turning into night

Naturally, like the dark - turning into light

Naturally, like the moon - mirroring the sun

Naturally, like the love - mirroring the peace

Sense all on offer, grateful in receipt
ease comes from being in the flow
trusting the process - observe, sense, repeat

Curiosity Of Expectation

Curiosity comes out to play - interest is peeked
expectations come out of hiding - havoc to reek

Not as obvious, not as loud
not as insistent but still as proud

In open observation, shoulds 'n' coulds run amok
hand-in-hand with small tuts, judgements and such

Words come to mind, unbidden, unneeded
on a smiling pause, slip into the silence, unspoken, unheeded

Curiosity may have killed the cat
but inner stillness confirms it's where our sanity's at

So Much

So much love, so much sadness
Don't push either away
Feel the sensations, energy, presence
Be curious of every tingle, churn, tightness and ache
Openly, cradling, comforting

So much love, holding space for all sensations
Without attachment to the mental space-invaders of
judgement, comparison and doubt
Enfolding all, in and of its making
Living, learning, evolving

So much love, waiting in earnest – recognise it
Don't turn away
Old stories, beliefs run deep
Sink into the silence, meet them in the depths
Seeing, realising, setting free

So much love, receiving and giving
Without attachment to personal and conceptual
In each breath, each sensed experience
Nuanced in beauty, enhanced in connections, shared in impermanence

So much love

Awake To More

Open our eyes to the experience of now
awake to more than a brand new day
vibration of the lips, tingling fingertips
observing sensation and thought, at play

No attachment to agitation
to thoughts of what could or should be
aware of life living, naturally giving
and from more than our eyes we will see

The clarity comes from an inner depth, a knowing
it fills us with a sense of peace, a quiet joy
as we rest in presence, one true essence
no superiority and separation to employ

We are infinite, living in finite form
allowing experiencing to simply take place
in wonder and pain, one and the same
awake to love and its everlasting embrace

Simply

Sink into the space
in and of creation
Simply aware, unperturbed, at ease

Aware of mind-body
through thought and sensation
Simply observing, with no desire to please

Observe all the layers
as they merge into one
Simply happening, which is life's way

Happening at will
no prize to be won
Simply being, at peace in one's day

Equal To Now

Freedom has no history
it is found in now
in being equal to all life has to offer

Freedom has no hopes and fears
it is found in integrity
in being equal to a life in flow

Freedom is our nature
it is found in love
in being equal to who we truly are

Freedom is to be love
it is found in Unity

More than a word
vibrating and resonating within – Love

Drawing us home with each new dawn
into a dimension, before and after time,
where experiencing takes the lead
resonance is our guiding force
and joy in presence, our default

Freedom is here
it is found in Eternity
in being equal to Now

Being ....

Be with the simplicity of life living
the breath in and out – life-giving
be swept on its breeze, as one with its blow
roll with its waves, at ease with its flow
as one with the dark, as we absorb its light
allowing its shifts, without a fight
harvest its seeds – sustenance from source
grateful in this presence, our true life force
and when the body inevitably tires and dies
continuance transpires within the mourner's cries
this presence never leaves merely takes a new form
as the breath, the wave, the rising dawn
smile into now and all it holds
in the simplest of acts, true love unfolds

Beyond The Mirror

Look in the mirror and
discover who you are,
concealed, yet longing to be seen

Look in the depths
know all you are
concealed by all you have been

Rest in this knowledge
behind all experiences sensed
where love comes to the fore

Sink into this love
behind perceptions and thought
where the idea of separation is no more

Look beyond the mirror
and know your true essence
revealed in awareness, revealed as presence

The Stillness Of Silence

When we trust in what we know
at one with our inner glow
the stillness of silence settles us so

Questioning all we perceive as real
abandoning commentary in order to feel
the stillness of silence helps us to heal

Releasing beliefs once held fast
no longer under the spell they cast
the stillness of silence embraces until at last

The doors of perception open wide
no sense of separation, no divide
the stillness of silence with our being collides

Resting in this place of knowing
aware of life, ebbing and flowing
the stillness of silence is us, love, growing

Live In The Knowledge

Live in the knowledge of who 'I' is
beyond all we learn we are not
beyond all we consider to be me and mine
recognising the true nature we forgot

We forgot as we lived the old paradigm
of separation and material might
believing only in logic's limitations
ignoring the heart's yearning to end our plight

Our plight of not being present for now
lost in thought and the promise this holds
Take a leaf of wisdom from nature's book
and experience life as it flows and unfolds

Flows and unfolds at a pace of its own
welcoming change and challenge as they arise
oblivious to the concepts of place and time
in the knowledge the 'I' never dies

Never dies just takes leave of the body
the personality celebrated yet no more
this realisation is the next evolution
a life-centric existence our saviour for sure

In All Its Glory

I am not my image or my story

I am consciousness living in all its glory

I am the cat, paws padding across the floor

I am this moment, no longer to ignore

I am the senses, and all they bequeath

I am the wind, blowing through the trees

I am the sun, shining oft'n behind the cloud

I am the observing, alone and in a crowd

I am the bird, gliding across the sky

I am eternity in a new born's eyes

I am the silence before the sound

I am the space in which all can be found

I am not my image or my story

I am life flowing now, in all its glory

The Ultimate Truth

Falling awake, we strip back the layers of relative truth
to reveal a knowing, stirring within, yet pervading all
speaking a language of its own
– full, enveloping, everlasting, complete

Nudging, coaxing, opening us to what life truly is
beyond all the stories and domestication

The mind is too close to see
but the heart, the heart understands,
lightens, lifts, opens to this new dimension

Vibrating as awareness itself
- love in all its expressions, in and as life,
Now – the ultimate truth

Equality In Presence

'Absence makes the heart grow fonder'
no surprise we feel such wonder
when all ignorance we put asunder
and rest in the truth of now

One consciousness, loving and kind
waiting within every seek yet never find
true nature is one – intertwined
a home-coming beyond any how

Bask in its radiance, the ordinary and the pain
giving and receiving without will to gain
equality in presence, the sun and the rain
effortless, in the knowing of thou

Timeless Now

The hard patina of separation
slowly cracks and crumbles
releasing, opening the heart like a flower
petal by petal, fulfilling its potential, its purpose
to blossom and thrive in Eternity – the timeless now

As naturally as a snake sheds its skin
a transformation occurs
the veils of past and future lift, surrendering us to life's flow
gratitude, synchronicities and beauty abound
the entire Universe rising and falling in us, as us - the timeless now

This is where desire drove us
desire to seek, to discover, to truly live
delivering us to this moment of connection and unity
the real treasures unearthed as we honour life in this understanding
we are everyone yet no-one, home – the timeless now

All Is As It Is

When living life in direct experience
through our senses and all this bequeaths
a peace settles in and around us
as the heart welcomes all it receives

Life in its diversity
reality beyond thoughts' push and pull
life in all its simplicity
often judged as ordinary, yet anything but dull

When living life in direct experience
being the sensations as they make themselves known
a quietness settles in and around us
as the seeds of knowing are lovingly sown

Life in its entirety
without the labels of good and bad
life in all its wonder
in the equality of happy and sad

When living life in direct experience
the illusion of separation slips away
compassion settles in and around us
as love pervades all, here to stay

Life in its profundity

natural intelligence too close to see

life in all its beauty

abide here and simply be

Looking Through These Eyes Of Love

Looking through these eyes of love
it's as though a soft focus lens has been applied
no finite edges separating one from another,
a continuous knowing, experiencing all in its presence
a pulsating, vibrating, awareness – in and of itself

Looking through these eyes of love
there's no drama, no sense of lack, simply life living
recognising this, abiding here, in our natural state
brings the very peace and happiness we seek
and it has been here, all along
waiting patiently for us to answer its call home,
in our own time, in our own way
to look through these eyes of love

Trust In All

Trust in all the heart has to say
it's our compass, our guiding light
moving, driving, propelling us on
as naturally as day precedes night

Shining in all, yet naked to the eye
it's the beacon illuminating the way
hearing, feeling, heeding the call
as naturally as night follows day

Questioning all our minds hold fast
it's knowing existence but not as a 'me'
breathing, sensing, experiencing life
as naturally as the earth births a tree

Accepting all, it is as it is
it's being true to awareness - the cosmic heart
living, loving, being in flow
as naturally as end follows starts

The Silence Knows Isness

(Dedicated to Jayne Pigford)

The silence knows isness
it is all that it knows

with words come concessions
some truth lost in the prose

To experience the stillness which silence draws near
is to experience isness – connected, we cohere

Let this experience expand, let it grow
let it be all that we know

No longer sucked in by the darkness of thought
no longer afraid to be other than we're taught

Open the heart and observe all with grace
open to pain, recognise the suffering we face

Eternity is ours, in the air which we breathe
eternity is connection, as we give and receive

Rest in the isness – serene, elate
rest in this, our natural state

All I am

Sit and feel into all I am
beyond the shadow of should

Breathe into all I am
beyond the trees to the wood

Settle into all I am
the whispers in the stillness alight

Rest into all I am
a knowing beyond eye-sight

Sink into all I am
the still point beyond compare

Living as all I am
now, presence, aware

Fall awake

Experience it all in a lifetime

It – who and what we truly are

Infinite treasures of love in all its expressions - compassion, gratitude, ease, joy, ecstasy, peace

This life is our playground, our place of learning, all these expressions our bounty to put into practice

to protect, nurture, nourish and they in turn, will return the favour, returning us to the one true state of who we are

- one with our surroundings and those we share this conceptual time and space with

This process is taking place whether we are aware or not but being aware, feeling it all, in its entirety, is to recognise these expressions as the treasures they truly are. The treasures we are, without the separation of me, me, me and the fear this state unleashes

Fall awake, experience it all in a lifetime,

it – who and what we truly are

Experience Heaven

We, the world, life itself exists
in this there is no dispute
but mind dreams up how all is perceived
thoughts and emotions too eagerly believed
leaving us disconnected, feeling separate, irresolute

There's no smoke 'n' mirrors, no puppet-master on high
just pure energy, alive, one source
consciousness empty, yet full to overflowing
of love, of wonder, of simply knowing
experience heaven in this, our life force

Behind Closed Lids

Discovery is offered behind closed lids
welcoming all the eye still sees
dancing, flickering candle flame
tonal shapes 'n' floating apostrophes

Settling into the wonder of now
letting be all sensation and thought
observing all for the transience it is
from these habits and patterns we are taught

No longer at the beck and call of emotion
lost in stories of judgement and doubt
open to experiencing all life has to offer
open to experiencing all life is about

Behind closed lids comes clarity
in the depths our true being is revealed
in the silence our inner wisdom speaks volumes
in stillness we find ourselves healed

of the sense of separation
of the limits our form dictates
of the belief in this, the illusion
of the very suffering to which fear relates

Open the lids and stay connected
be awake to life as it flows
abide as one - awareness
abide as that which knows

Sanctuary Within

We observe with awareness, the awareness within
to experience now and all of its gifts
any anxiety – sensations to be felt then released
on this path of no path, something shifts

As we connect with the sanctuary, the sanctuary within
a sense of gratitude arises and extends
the loving stillness within, observing the loving stillness without
and the limitations and suffering this transcends

When experienced with reverence, the reverence within
our minds and bodies shine as one, in unity
basking in the gratitude, this recognition brings
in this, our true presence, we are free

Experience Existence

See yourself in a raindrop
as it falls from a cloud with ease
hear yourself in a rustling leaf
as it dances to the song of the breeze
smell yourself in a clump of earth
as it's turned over to meet with the air
taste yourself in a grain of salt
as it dissolves into this moment to share
feel yourself in this raindrop,
this leaf, this earth, this grain of salt
in this oneness we experience existence
a knowing in which to exalt

Slip Into Silence

Settle into practice
aware of breathing as the body receives, and then gives
back into the space it cometh
back into the space where all lives

Settle into practice
open to welcome all that may arise, and then fall
back into the space it cometh
back into the space of us all

Slip into silence
the inner silence where the truth will be revealed
emitting from the space it cometh
emitting from the space we are healed

Slip into silence
its warm embrace allowing all to be, as it is
emitting from the space it cometh
emitting from the space true love lives

Slip further
into its stillness where peace and serenity, gently wait
returning us to the space we cometh
returning us to the space to relate

Slip further

into its welcome where knowing permeates all, to our core

returning us to the space we cometh

returning us to the space, t'fear no more

Be The Light

Out of the darkness comes the light
taking its place in this world
like the day progresses, moment by moment,
bringing forth the dusk and the dawn
so the light emerges from the dark
shining its infinite glory

Out of the silence comes the truth
taking its place in this world.
like the whisper of the wind as it moves through the trees
highlighting our oneness with nature
settle into the silence and all it reveals
sharing its infinite love

Out of the present comes the awareness
taking its place in this world
like the water flowing, surrendering to its course
in awareness we are all that we are
at one with our senses, no illusion, absolute
connecting to its infinite joy

Out of the awareness comes the compassion

taking its place in this world.

like the sun shining bright, even behind the cloud

never striving, just being what it is

compassion is our true essence

bringing its infinite peace

I Am

Sink into the welcoming space
At once recognised
Home, I am

Sink into the limitless emptiness
Feel its embrace
Peace, I am

Sink into the expanse of knowing
Experiencing all equally
Happiness, I am

Sink into the nourishing void
Sustenance from source
Love, I am

Recognising One As All

Surrender to now
as the illusion slips away

Be present in wisdom and knowing

True to now
as the concepts fall away

Be the seeds after sowing

Radiate in now
as one turns towards all

Be pure energy to-ing and fro-ing

Rest in now
recognising one as all

Be the expression of consciousness flowing

This Peace

Pure consciousness delivers us from our knowing state
into the joy of a brand new day
this peace we feel in our restful sleep
soon hijacked by thought, slips away

It is this peace we want to rediscover
this peace with which we want to reconnect
in this peace there is a real sense of home-coming
receiving sustenance from our source direct

This sustenance, the essence of who we are
pure love in its simplest form
the only lack – that of separation
without which we can weather any storm

This separation just part of the illusion
a veil created from perception, thought and belief
when united in pure consciousness, the un-distracted,
welcome this peace with a sigh of relief

To reach it we must say goodbye to the drama
goodbye to the judgement, the conflict and the doubt
trust in oneness, our own presence
whose infinite wisdom we cannot do without

Heart of All

I am the heart of all
at the heart of all
within the heart of all

Let all perceptions, opinions be swallowed by
this awareness, this knowing, this inner cry

Be love and trust in its power
immersion in now, beyond any hour

Joy to joy, peace to peace
attraction vibrates within every release

All possibilities await in uncertainty
live in the heart, know eternity

Go Inside. Go Inside

Go inside. Go inside
where there is no-one
in solitude, yet not alone

Go inside. Go inside
touched by earth and sun
in the familiar and yet unknown

Go inside. Go inside
where light sees dark
in stillness, clarity transpires

Go inside. Go inside
touched by breath's spark
in abandon, courage inspires

Go inside. Go inside
where all is revealed
in wisdom, beyond intellect

Go inside. Go inside
touched by tree and field
in beauty, beyond perfect

Go inside. Go inside
touched by rivers and streams
in gratitude of this - existence

Go inside. Go inside
where change convenes
in recognition of life's impermanence

Behind The Curtain

Paintbrush or pen in hand
marathon run or combing the sand

Not miles away, very much here
in the flow, beyond identity and fear

Stepping from behind the curtain
questioning all we believe to be certain

Thoughts, sensations - only part of the show
not given title credits over the reality we know

Caught up in the quiet joy of now
natural response to all we allow

Only Now

What went before
is no more

What could be
is not reality

Aware of what's real
all sensations to feel

Thoughts to observe
as the 'me, me, me' they serve

Watch the chitter-chatter
reach the heart of the matter

Taking leave of your senses
leads to a life of pretences

Compassion starts here
as authenticity draws near

In this knowing
life is simply flowing

Stop ruminating on "why and how"
know there is only now

The Greatest Show

Be the kindest kind of kind
leave ideas of separation and old stories behind
lead with the heart, balancing body and mind
be the mirror of life and see what you find

Reflections of beauty beyond time and place
one with the stillness, its fullness, its space
a love for all, felt with gratitude and grace
expressed in every action, like a warm embrace

This truth, like the Sun, is always here
never dimmed, just hidden, behind clouds of fear
trust in Mother Earth's nature, nearer than near
love life for what it is, in the clear and unclear

Trust compassion is grown from the smallest of seed
know joy is found – not in want but in deed
truly listen as inner wisdom is the voice to heed
experience each honoured breath as inspiration is freed

Inspiration to live fully, creating as we go
living in service to life itself, by being its flow
in the understanding we are so much more than we know
we are inter-beings in and of Life – the Greatest Show!

Love ....

It is said, it is all around us
and that it's all we need
it is a many splendored thing
and it's the energy on which we feed

We know it as a power
it's called crazy, young and true
it can be found in the time of cholera
and in a cold climate too

It's all of these things and yet so much more
it reconnects, restores, sets us free
it's not just a romantic thing between two
and blocking it from life's no way to be

Let it lift us and let it rise us above
all adversity, don't react, respond in style
we can be the carrier, share it wide
'cos it's infectious and touching, like a smile

So remember, it's all around us
and that it's all we need
it's the essence of each and everyone
and where compassion 'n' kindness take the lead

Life's Rich Tapestry

The ever-present 'I am'
like a spool of golden thread,
constantly unravelling,
weaves through the Universal tapestry
to rest in its masterpiece

Too close to see the big picture
but when settled in the knowing
awareness itself
the intricacies of each stitch
are appreciated in gratitude and wonder

The loving light of the golden thread
naturally inter-twining, this way and that,
recognises itself
in each and every stitch
illuming as it goes

Carefree of looping, or changing pattern
the precious golden thread
laces free
over and under the fabric of life
experiencing each movement as the gift it is

And when the conditions are such

each golden thread rewinds into the spool

into itself, of the masterpiece

infinite embroidery

continuing to create life's rich tapestry

Precious In Its Presence

Pink tinged sky on a winter's morn
from which the golden rose of silence
blooms and blossoms in the stillness
- precious in its presence

Petals open within the gift of being
short-lived yet eternal
drooping yet ever present
- carpeting the path of no path

Spiky thorns, offering protection, run deep
vital yet not all-consuming
prickly yet not a threat
- fertilising all resilience

The light of the golden rose
rests in the freedom of now
inclusive, in its expanse
- precious in its presence

Collaborators Of Peace

Our refuge, our haven is only a breath away
as we follow its flow, its lead
its natural rhythm, taking us into its depths
in the stillness, the silence we heed

Valuing, honouring, the simplicities of now
Universal, yet appear personal in their receipt
held in this companionable, supportive space
in whose strength, heart to heart, we meet

From here, in shared silence we discover all we are
awakening from all we are not
sensing the vital essence, of one and all
in the recognition, this essence will never stop

Embodying this understanding, we are expressions of love
generous and courteous as we share
healing together, collaborators of peace
in community – a unity, beyond compare

Last Day Before Spring

The last day of winter, low sunshine radiating,
dazzling - thanking this season for all it offered

Dormancy, hibernation,
rest and recuperation,
hidden preparations for the spectacle soon to be revealed

Trees - majestic, reaching out to the great unknown
buds on skeletal canopies, standing out like goose-pimples on shivery skin
signalling the soon to be seen robes of green

As the earth births new growth from the ground and seed-trays alike,
blossom blooms on neighbouring shrubs 'n' trees
welcomed by the lingering colour of winter stalwarts and early risers

Birds industriously collect fallen twigs, peeling bark,
gathering moss from lawns and tree stumps
lovingly creating a home from which to welcome new life

Earthworms preparing soil, insects preparing to eat and be eaten
bees 'n' butterflies waking up to pollinate and propagate - life's essentials
cool, fresh air caresses all in its path,
pairing with the sun's heat to dry out the previous days sustaining rain
- elemental magic

We too, stretch, exercise, shed the winter gain,

feel the energy of this change

read it, be it, as we tune into the sensory wonder of now

The last day before Spring

low sunshine, radiating, dazzling

- sharing the promise of all this season brings

Knowing Now

There's a stirring inside, driving us on
delivering us to the truth we seek
too radical, too close for the mind to grasp
it takes courage to learn a language without speech

In the stillness and silence we investigate
then investigate and investigate some more
no 'one' to be found - behind eyes, in head
no boundaries between the foot and the floor

Only sensations, arising and falling in space
fulfilling, as we sink into its expanse
settling into wholeness, no longer contracted, wound tight
an understanding beyond belief and mere chance

The senses, always on, allowing experiencing to take place
simply happening as the right conditions deem it so
no individual to be found with remote control in hand
no decider of when the wind doth blow

Free of the idea, of being this illusory me
the form we take is recognised as that known
an energetic expression, a wonder of life
no 'me' or 'my life' to own

Liberation is found here, in unconditional love
the light of knowing – as babes we knew how
don't wait to leave this form to return to this state
fall awake and be knowing now

One More Illusion

Footsteps on the deserted pavement tap out the rhythm of the night

as a shower of autumn rain leaves a glistening dew on its surface

street lights highlight miniature pools, an accumulation of tiny droplets awaiting dispersion

as the footsteps approach - kicking, flicking into the space of night

Her smoky eyes watch him from her elevated position

the broken silence of life drawing her out

she ponders his existence, his mood, his gait

the lone figure - an air of peace and ease – hand in hand with the present

As if to prove her right, he stops,

tilts his head, looks into the dark depths of the road

smiling wistfully as he watches the reflection of traffic lights changing unbidden,

their colours dancing, sparkling actors on the screen of tarmac

She can see how far he is from the angry man of a year ago

his thoughts then full of shoulds and coulds

weights and measures, assumptions of what would be

searching for those assurances of life, in guises of hope and expectancy

He walks on, picks up his pace, now aware of the onset of tiredness

- reminding him of the hour –

a feeling made up of sensations - like his anger - to be acknowledged, felt

no story-telling with its victims and recriminations

She knows he senses her, on the periphery of his awareness

there was a time he would welcome her in an open embrace

take her to heart - it would be her hand he held

always fun – well for her, at least

As he reaches for his garden gate, anticipating the touch of cool

wet wood beneath his fingers

he turns, her desire penetrating the air around

knocking hard at the door of his resolve

he wishes her next conquest well

She too smiles ruefully

in his knowing he is lost to her

it's time for her to take her leave

her short dark wings unfurl behind her

Tuning into the chatter of the next mind to stir

delivery of disappointment in her sights

one more illusion in a life of what if

the Daemon of Expectation takes flight

Remember Now

As he makes his way across the sand
footprints mark his progress in its firmness
hurrying to the water to feel part of something more
to ease this overwhelming feeling of aloneness

the coolness of its touch, garners a response
he's unsure whether to stay or to flee
he pauses awhile, as it laps around his feet
and takes this opportunity to simply be

the seaweed stirs and catches
around his feet, between his toes
resembling thoughts, flowing and snagging
their persistence his greatest foes

his training had prepared him for battle
for fighting enemies, known and seen
but the one now raging inside him
had him reaching for the amphetamines

his steps take him deeper and deeper
where the seaweed, like his thoughts, thin out
its depth welcoming, inviting
releasing tension, sadness, self-doubt

as his head slips under the water
there comes a still and silent embrace
offering a peace long sought after
an opportunity to come face to face

with the daemons replaying their stories
of all that had gone before
the bloodshed, the pain, the aching loss,
and of all the horrors left in store

but as he sinks further into the silence
the daemons dissolve into the deep
the beauty witnessed in this stillness
replacing all he believed was his to keep

as he floats back to the surface
experiencing from a fresh pair of eyes
even to his breath he feels connected
and in the familiar there is no disguise

once again he feels part of something bigger
no longer him and his thoughts against the world
the seaweed like these thoughts no longer clinging
allowing a willingness to be with life as it unfurls

he steps back into the shallows

alive to all his senses allow

compassion for his fellow fighters

in their memory he'll live on, in the now

Wonderful Moment

Alive to this feeling, this breath, this sound
trees cast their spell, in this arboreal surround
beauty, connection in the seen and unseen
recognised by the heart, in our cells and our genes

Wistful, peaceful - a contentment restored
a one-ness turned towards, no longer ignored
footfall grounding to Mother Earth in this moment
a smile of home-coming, what a wonderful moment

Ask Ourselves Why?

Why have we come so far,
so far away from who we truly are?

The constant distractions from the here and now
the thoughts and beliefs that convince us how
we are separate subjects in our own little realm
not even aware it's the chattering mind at the helm

A virus can bring our world to a stand-still
but the distractions go on; we still maim and kill
anger is born from a deep sense of fear
of the very death this behaviour brings near

A murder most foul is captured on screen
so we let our anger boil over and vent our spleen
violence and vitriol become the order of the day
Why have we come so far, so far away?

Or we sit and hang our heads in shame
is our antipathy to our sisters and brothers to blame?
do we really try to understand their plight
or get defensive and glove-up, ready for a fight?

Why is it ok to lash out and hate?

it's not, it's not, it's just sealing our fate
anger is an emotion, allowed to be felt
but as a sensation within, not a blow to be dealt

Whichever side you find yourself on
ask yourself why you feel this anger so strong?
when you do and the answer is authentic and true
you'll discover the source of anger is in you

So old stories of superiority, must be learned, are just that
- stories and old, no basis in fact
'Who do they think they are?' thoughts and beliefs rage on
Where, oh where, has all the love gone?

Well the love is still here, it's just shielded by
the labels, masks and stories we rate so high
by the comparisons and judgements we hold so dear
and by the belief in separation – our real fear

But we can begin again, in universal unity
the planet and all its inhabitants, an earthly equality
just take time to go within, sit awhile, be still
and discover love is our essence, non-separation our will

The Boot On The Hill

She packed up a few necessities
and made her way to the door
stopping for one last backward glance
at the room she'd see no more

It'd always been the heart of the home
where she cooked, read by the fire, even slept
more so over the last few months
as her stair-climbing became less adept

Both her children had spent many a day
growing in and out of this space
The memories filled her heart and her mind
a warm smile spread over her face

She turned on her heel, without regret
the end, she knew, was near
there was one last thing left to do
on where she would go she was clear

She climbed aboard her transport then
she'd only need to walk the last few feet
when she reached the top of the hillside
and lay down for her maker to meet

As she turned the key in the ignition
she experienced such a sheer sense of fun
her children, still shocked, thought her crazy
for buying a quad bike at eighty-one!

Her grandchildren, on the other hand
thought it extremely cool, hip, whatever it is they now said
some even with off-spring of their own
more in touch with the heart than the head

The destination was one of her favourites
her husband of 52 years had loved it too
but he had passed now more than 10 years ago
it was the place he'd first said 'I Love You'

She emptied her bag of its contents
and changed from wellies into her elegant ankle boots
the cheese and wine she was going to savour
as she listened out for the owls courting hoots

Dusk was steadily drawing to a close
the spring night sky, soon to be found
providing a backdrop to the moon and the stars
as she lay her blanket out on the ground

Her breaths were growing steadily weaker
as she lay prone, looking up to the sky
the same sky they had danced and sung under
the last scene for her to view, before she die

As the stars flickered and sparkled above her
his hand seemed to magically appear
the youth from all those years ago
was once again miraculously here

Her younger self took the proffered hand
and in the moonlight they started to spin
the hillside their dance floor, the moon their guiding light
pure joy lit up their souls from within

Then, he clicked his fingers and down from the sky
a star slipped in real close to release
ribbons of stardust creating a swing
which he lifted her upon with ease

She swung on that star for what seemed an hour
her life playing out before her eyes
the pain and the pleasure, all a part of its gift
pure love, leaving no room for disguise

……..

She was found the very next morning
lying on her blanket on the ground
her life-force was no longer present
one ankle boot was never to be found

But when you stand at a distance and admire
the countryside, its beauty far and wide
you'll see where the local flora and fauna
bound part of her to forever reside

Farewell To Illusion

The time has come to go our separate ways

I'd liked to say 'you served me well' but that would be a lie
or at least a half-truth

Another of those false-positives

which for so long kept this day at bay

where I would know your goading was not all I am

but still I would sink into the delusion

fear of the unknown keeping me in purgatory

lost in you and the promises you held

but the dawning grew and became full daylight

no more scaredy-cat, hiding in the shadows, stretched, distorted

in the prolonged story-telling

Freedom - freedom is here, with all labels of 'yours' and 'mine' shed in
the alleyways

I aspire to live in the light of what is

and rejoice in the knowledge the world never was flat

Acknowledgements

I came to mindfulness in 2015 after a friend recommended I read "The Power of the Sub-Conscious Mind" by Joseph Murphy. I was about to take a year out of employment to build up a body of artwork before taking it to market and was full of self-doubt and self-criticism. This book was perfect, as it talks of how not to believe all the old stories of what we can and cannot do. **Thank you, Lilibeth Gonzalez-Lee**, for pointing me in the right direction.

Though I didn't know it as mindfulness immediately, the book made me hungry to discover more. This led me to Hay House Publications and its plethora of authors – **Louise Hay, Drs Wayne Dyer and Robert Holden and Gabby Bernstein** to name but a few. **Thank you all!** I soon realised the common theme in these teachings was being present/mindful. So I took a formal online 8 week MBSR course and was hooked. For someone who had suffered bouts of clinical depression over the years, to learn I was not my thoughts, they weren't real or mine was a revelation and something I wanted to teach others.

In 2018 following completion of an MBCT teacher training course - **Thank you Dr Patrizia Collard** – I attended a weekend retreat with the renowned five-time author and international teacher, Suryacitta, The Happy Buddha. Here I was introduced to the art of simplifying mindfulness not only from a teaching point of view but in respect of my own practice. So much of what Surya said resonated with me and this is when the poetry really started to flow. In the knowledge we are not trying to get anywhere in meditation, simply being at one with the isness of life, it was not surprising the poetry soon sang with non-dual understanding. Out of the head and into the heart - one heart: the heart of life.

I am honoured that Suryacitta – teacher, mentor, friend – offered to write the introduction to this book of poems. **Thank you, Suryacitta, for so much more than this Introduction.**

I continue to write, read, teach and learn from poetry, in the wonder of the flow of natural intelligence with no 'me' to take credit.

Samantha Hall

www.hallofmindfulness.co.uk

Printed in Great Britain
by Amazon